Sports Alive!

Roller Hockey

by Charles and Linda George

Consultant:
Mike Zaidman
Director and Curator
National Museum of Roller Skating

CAPSTONE BOOKS
an imprint of Capstone Press
Mankato, Minnesota

Capstone Books are published by Capstone Press
151 Good Counsel Drive, P.O. Box 669, Mankato, Minnesota 56002
http://www.capstone-press.com

Library of Congress Cataloging-in-Publication Data
George, Charles, 1949–
   Roller hockey/by Charles and Linda George.
   p. cm.—(Sports alive!)
   Includes bibliographical references (p. 45) and index.
   Summary: Describes the history, equipment, techniques, and rules of roller
hockey.
   ISBN 0-7368-0053-0
   1. Roller hockey—Juvenile literature. [1. Roller hockey. 2. Hockey.]
I. George, Linda. II. Title. III. Series.
GV859.7.G46 1999
796.21—dc21
                                                                98-17217
                                                                     CIP
                                                                      AC

Editorial Credits
Mark Drew, editor; Clay Schotzko/Icon Productions, cover designer;
   Sheri Gosewisch, photo researcher

Photo Credits
Corbis-Bettmann, 10
Davis Barber, 33, 37, 42
John Lyman, 7, 8, 14, 20, 23, 26, 30, 34, 38, 41
Kim Karpeles, 24–25
Landmark Stock Exchange/John Lyman, cover, 4, 29
National Museum of Roller Skating, 13
Rob Miracle, 19
Shelly Castellano, 16

Table of Contents

Chapter 1

Roller Hockey

Roller hockey is closely related to the sport of ice hockey. Both roller hockey and ice hockey are team sports played on rectangular surfaces known as rinks. A goal with a net stands at each end of roller hockey and ice hockey rinks.

Two teams compete in roller hockey and ice hockey games. Players in both sports use ice hockey sticks to move a flat disk called a puck over the rink. The object of roller hockey and ice hockey games is to hit the puck into the opposing team's goal.

Roller Hockey and Ice Hockey Differences

Roller hockey differs from ice hockey in several important ways. People can play roller hockey

Two teams compete in roller hockey games.

on almost any hard surface. People play roller hockey on playgrounds and empty parking lots. They play roller hockey on concrete floors inside buildings. People also play on rinks made just for roller hockey.

People do not always use a puck to play roller hockey. Players sometimes use a special low-bounce ball. The use of a puck or a ball depends on the playing surface.

Another major difference between ice hockey and roller hockey is the skates. Roller hockey players use roller skates instead of ice skates. Roller skates make ice hockey-style hockey playable on surfaces other than ice.

Some people use quad skates to play roller hockey. Quad skates have two pairs of wheels on each boot. One pair of wheels is beneath the heel of the boot. The other pair is beneath the toe. A rod called an axle connects to the center of each wheel in a pair. These axles allow the wheels to spin.

Most people use in-line skates for roller hockey. In-line skates have two or more wheels mounted in a straight line under each boot.

Roller hockey is a fast sport.

Roller Hockey Basics

Roller hockey is a fast sport. Players must continuously adjust to new situations as they speed up and down the rink. They must dodge other players as they race for the puck or ball. They must think and act quickly as they move the puck or ball toward the opposing team's goal.

Goalies try to prevent the puck or ball from entering their team's goal.

Each team in a roller hockey game has four skaters and a goalie on the rink. A team receives one point when its players hit the puck or ball into the opposing team's goal. The team with the most points at the end of the game wins.

The team that controls the puck or ball is on offense. Four offensive skaters try to advance the puck or ball toward the opposing team's goal. Skaters dribble the puck or ball to move it down the rink. They dribble by tapping the puck or ball with the blades of their sticks as they skate. Skaters also pass the puck or ball to their teammates. Offensive skaters attempt to score when they get near the opposing team's goal.

The team that does not control the puck or ball is on defense. Defensive skaters try to gain control of the puck or ball. They attempt to stop passes and steal the puck or ball. Defensive skaters try to poke the puck or ball away from offensive skaters. Roller hockey players call this a poke check. Skaters on defense also try to block the opposing team's shots.

Goalies usually play defense. They stay in front of their team's goal throughout the game. Goalies try to prevent the puck or ball from entering their team's goal. They do this by blocking shots with their bodies, sticks, and skates. They also use special goalie's equipment to block shots.

Chapter 2

The History of Roller Hockey

Roller hockey came from the sports of field hockey and ice hockey. Field hockey started in Asia about 4,000 years ago. The sport later spread to Europe. The English organized field hockey into its current form. Field hockey came to North America in the late 1800s.

Two teams of eleven people compete in field hockey. The teams play on rectangular sections of flat, grassy land. Players run after a small leather ball and strike it with canes. Each cane has a hook-shaped end called a crook. Players try to hit the ball into the opposing team's goal.

People played the first official game of ice hockey in 1855. A Canadian named W. F. Robertson created the rules for ice hockey. He adapted field hockey rules for play on ice.

Roller hockey came from the sports of field hockey and ice hockey.

Ice hockey teams have six players. Players skate after a hard rubber puck instead of a small, leather ball. They strike the puck with sticks. Ice hockey sticks are longer than field hockey canes. The sticks also have slightly curved blades on one end instead of crooks.

Roller Skates and Roller Hockey

An Englishman named Joseph Merlin created the first roller skates around 1760. No one is sure what his skates looked like. Many experts believe that Merlin's roller skates were most likely in-line skates.

Experts do know that a Frenchman named M. Petitbled made the first officially recognized in-line skates in 1819. Petitbled's skates each had three wood, metal, or ivory wheels attached to a wood plate. Skaters fastened the plates to their feet with leather straps.

In 1863, an American named James L. Plimpton created the earliest version of today's quad skates. Plimpton's skates each had two pairs of wood wheels attached to a wood plate. Plimpton's roller skates were very popular

People started to organize roller skating sports in the late 1800s.

because they allowed skaters to turn easily. They were so popular that people nearly forgot about in-line skates. Plimpton's roller skates also made roller skating more popular.

People started to organize roller skating sports in the late 1800s. They first played a type of roller hockey in England in 1878. The game was similar to field hockey.

Today's version of roller hockey began after Scott and Brennan Olson created modern in-line roller skates.

No one is certain when people began using ice hockey sticks and pucks to play roller hockey. But experts believe it was sometime between 1930 and 1940. Soon after, people were playing ice hockey-style roller hockey in roller rinks, streets, and parking lots.

Roller Hockey Today

Today's version of roller hockey began after Scott and Brennan Olson created modern in-line roller skates. The Olson brothers were ice hockey players. They wanted to find a way to practice ice hockey during summer. In-line skates perform more like ice skates than quad skates do.

In 1980, the Olson brothers found a pair of in-line skates in a sporting goods store. The Chicago Roller Skate Company had built the skates in 1966. The skates had four rubber wheels attached to each boot. But the boots were not very sturdy. So the Olsons decided to change the design of the skates.

The Olson brothers mounted the wheels onto a pair of leather ice hockey boots. The ice hockey boots were stiffer and provided more ankle support than the skates' original boots. The Olsons also added a rubber brake pad to the rear of each skate.

The popularity of ice hockey-style roller hockey rapidly grew after the Olsons built their skates. The Olsons' skates also helped make in-line skating one of the fastest growing sports in North America.

 Chapter 3

Equipment and Safety

Roller hockey equipment is similar to the equipment used for ice hockey. Basic equipment includes skates and sticks. Roller hockey players also wear helmets and other protective gear.

Skates

Roller skates are one of the most important pieces of roller hockey equipment. People wear either quad skates or in-line skates to play roller hockey. Most people prefer in-line skates. They find that in-line skates are lighter and sturdier than quad skates.

People can use just about any type of in-line skates to play roller hockey. But in-line skates specially made for roller hockey are safest. People must be able to bend their ankles to play

Basic roller hockey equipment includes skates, sticks, helmets, and other protective gear.

roller hockey. In-line roller hockey skates are more flexible than other types of in-line skates.

In-line roller hockey skates look similar to ice hockey skates. The boots are usually leather and have laces. But some in-line roller hockey boots are plastic. Plastic boots normally have buckles instead of laces. Players who need more ankle support often use plastic skates. Leather skates are more flexible than plastic skates.

Wheels

Wheels for both quad and in-line roller hockey skates come in different levels of hardness. The hardness of the wheels affects how long they last. Soft wheels wear out faster than hard wheels. Hardness also affects how well players can move on their skates. Soft wheels provide more grip than hard wheels. Players use hard wheels when they play on rough concrete or blacktop. They use soft wheels when they play on smooth surfaces.

Experienced roller hockey players who use in-line skates often rocker their wheels. They place the front and back wheels slightly higher

Roller hockey pucks have small plastic buttons called nibbles on their surfaces. Nibbles help pucks glide.

than the two middle wheels. This makes it easier for players to make tight turns. But skates with rockered wheels are not as stable as skates with level wheels.

Pucks, Balls, and Sticks

Roller hockey players play with either a roller hockey puck or a ball. Roller hockey pucks are hard plastic disks. Many pucks have small plastic buttons called nibbles on their surfaces

Roller hockey players use the same sticks that ice hockey players use.

to help them glide. Roller hockey balls are made from strong, low-bounce rubber. Pucks perform best on smooth surfaces such as plastic or painted wood. Players prefer to use balls on rough surfaces such as blacktop parking lots.

Roller hockey sticks have long shafts with slightly curved blades at one end. Hockey sticks come in several different lengths. Stick length depends on the size of the hockey player. But sticks cannot be longer than 62 inches (157 centimeters) from the top to the end of the shaft. Blades can be no longer than 12 and one-half inches (32 centimeters).

Roller hockey sticks are made from a variety of materials. Players generally prefer sticks with wood shafts and blades when they play on smooth surfaces. Rough surfaces often cause wood blades to wear down and split apart. Sticks with plastic or fiberglass blades are better for play on rough surfaces. Fiberglass is a strong, lightweight material made from fine threads of glass. Both plastic and fiberglass resist wear better than wood.

Protective Equipment

Roller hockey is a risky sport. The puck or ball travels quickly and often hits players. Players accidentally hit one another with their sticks. They sometimes skate into one another and fall onto the hard playing surface.

Most roller hockey players wear protective equipment to prevent injuries. Many leagues require players to wear full protective gear. Full protective gear includes mouth guards and helmets with full face shields. It also includes knee and shin guards, elbow pads, gloves, and hockey pants.

Goalies' Equipment

Goalies must wear additional equipment for protection from the puck or ball. They sometimes wear a standard helmet with a full face cage. But goalies usually wear a goalie's helmet. A goalie's helmet is larger than a standard helmet and protects all areas of the head.

Goalies wear many pads and protectors to avoid being injured by a puck or ball. They wear upper-arm pads, shoulder pads, and large leg pads. Protective gear also includes thick chest protectors. Goalies wear a goalkeeper's glove on one hand and a blocker on the other. A blocker is a rectangular pad that goalies use to stop a puck or ball.

Goalies' sticks are different from the sticks that other players use. A goalie's stick blade is longer than the blade of a skater's stick. It can be

A goalie's helmet is larger than a standard helmet.

up to 15 and one-half inches (39 centimeters) long. The shaft of a goalie's stick also is wider at the bottom than the shaft of a skater's stick. The wider shaft helps goalies stop shots.

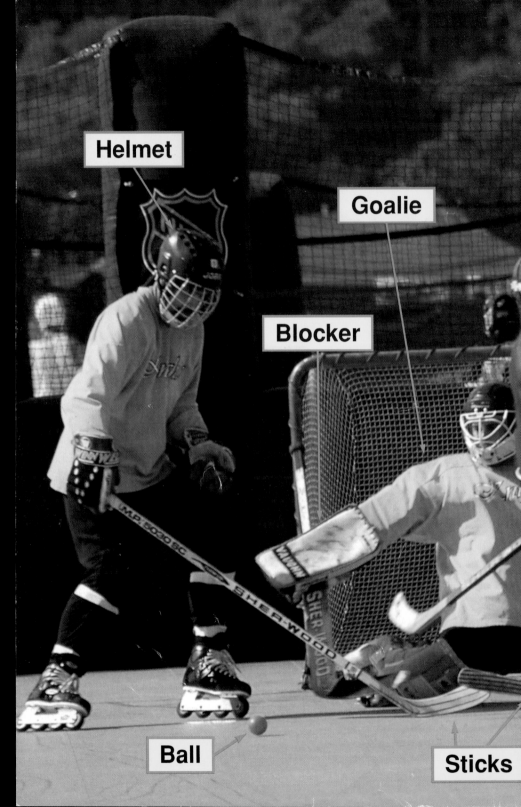

Helmet

Goalie

Blocker

Ball

Sticks

Forward

Goal

Defender

In-Line Skates

Chapter 4

Skills and Techniques

Roller hockey players need to master several basic skills before they can compete in games. Players must know how to handle their sticks. They must know how to move, pass, and shoot the puck or ball. Players also must be good roller skaters.

Roller skating is perhaps the most important skill for roller hockey players to master. Players must be able to skate rapidly both forward and backward. They must be able to make quick starts, sudden stops, and sharp turns. Players should be able to move as well on skates as they can in shoes. To become good skaters, players spend much of their practice time working on skating techniques.

Roller hockey players must know how to move, pass, and shoot the puck or ball.

Stickhandling

Stickhandling is almost as important as skating. Good stickhandlers know how to control and move the puck or ball with their hockey sticks. Players first need to learn how to hold their sticks before they can become good stickhandlers.

Players usually place one hand just below the top of the shaft. They place the other hand six to 12 inches (15 to 30 centimeters) below the top hand. The grip of the lower hand is somewhat loose. Players slide this hand down before shooting. This increases the power of players' shots.

Good stickhandlers know how to use their sticks to dribble the puck or ball around the rink. The two methods of dribbling are side-to-side and front-to-back.

Players keep the puck or ball in front of them when they use the side-to-side method. They tap the puck or ball back and forth with their sticks as they skate. This is the best method for controlling the puck or ball when skating forward quickly.

Players move the puck or ball to their sides when they use the front-to-back method. They then sweep the puck or ball forward and catch it with their sticks. Players often use this method

Roller hockey players keep the puck in front of them when using the side-to-side dribbling method.

when they skate slowly. The front-to-back method helps players set up passes and shots.

Passing

Passing is another basic skill that roller hockey players must master. The fastest way to move the puck or ball on the playing surface is to pass it. Players must be able to control exactly where the puck or ball goes when they make passes.

Roller hockey players pass the puck ahead or to the side with a forehand pass.

Players use three basic passes in roller hockey. They are the forehand pass, the backhand pass, and the flip pass. Players pass the puck or ball ahead or to the side with a forehand pass. They pass the puck or ball behind or to the side with a backhand pass. Players use a smooth sweeping motion to send the puck or ball to a teammate.

Flip passes usually are short passes. Players use their sticks to lift the puck or ball off the playing surface with flip passes. They then flip the puck or ball over defenders' sticks.

Shooting

Shooting is an important part of roller hockey players' offensive game. Good shooters try to make quick, powerful, and accurate shots. Good shooters also pick their shots carefully. They look for areas of the goal left open by the goalie. They then shoot the puck or ball toward those open areas.

Players use four basic types of shots. These are the wrist shot, the backhand shot, the slap shot, and the flip shot. The type of shot players choose depends on the situation.

The wrist shot is similar to the forehand pass. Players use a sweeping motion to send the puck or ball toward the goal. But the sweeping motion for the wrist shot is quicker and more forceful than for the forehand pass. Players snap their wrists just before releasing the puck or ball.

This gives extra power to the shot. Players attempt wrist shots from anywhere in front of the goal. Many players believe the wrist shot is the most accurate type of shot.

The backhand shot is much like the backhand pass and the wrist shot. Players sweep the puck or ball with the back side of a stick's blade. This shot is usually not as powerful as the wrist shot. Players use this shot when they are a short distance from the goal.

Players use a full swing for slap shots. They bring their sticks back while sliding their lower hands down the shaft. They then swing their sticks down and hit the puck or ball hard.

The slap shot is a powerful shot. But it is not a very accurate shot. Players usually use the slap shot when they are far from the goal.

Flip shots are similar to flip passes. Players scoop the puck or ball off the surface with the blades of their sticks. They then flip the puck or ball over defenders' sticks and toward the goal. Players often use flip shots when the goalie is on the ground.

Players use a full swing for slap shots.

Chapter 5

The Game

Roller hockey teams can have up to 12 players. But only five players from each team can be on the rink during a game. Four of the players on a team are skaters. Skaters play both offense and defense throughout a game. The remaining player is a goalie.

Each player on a roller hockey team plays one of three basic positions. The positions are forward, defender, and goalie. Each position in roller hockey is important. The skills that players need vary for each position.

Forwards

A roller hockey team usually has two forwards on the rink. They are often the team's best skaters, stickhandlers, and shooters. Forwards

Skaters play both offense and defense throughout a roller hockey game.

also are good passers. Forwards usually play offense. But they must play defense when the other team controls the puck or ball. Forwards try to steal the puck when on defense.

The main role of forwards is to create scoring opportunities. To do this, they move the puck into the opposing team's zone. Forwards then look to see if they have a clear shot at the other team's goal. If they have a clear shot, forwards try to shoot the puck or ball past the goalie. Forwards who do not have a clear shot pass the puck or ball to a teammate.

Players need to be in excellent shape to be forwards. Forwards are always moving. They skate the length of the rink at full speed many times during a game.

Defenders

A roller hockey team also has two defenders on the rink. Defenders play much of the game near their own goal. Their main role is to prevent opposing forwards from scoring. Defenders try to break up offensive plays by intercepting passes. They try to make opponents take long shots or shots from poor angles.

Defenders play much of the game near their own goal. They try to prevent opposing forwards from scoring.

Defenders must be good skaters and stickhandlers. They spend most of their time skating with the opposing team's forwards. Defenders often skate backward in front of forwards while forwards move down the rink. This allows defenders to see what the forwards are doing. Skating backward also allows defenders to block the forwards' views of the goal.

Defenders play offense when they gain control of the puck or ball. Defenders usually pass the puck or ball to their team's forwards. Defenders sometimes dribble the puck or ball toward the opposing team's goal and take a shot. Most defenders take slap shots. Slap shots allow defenders to remain in position to defend their own goal.

Goalies

The fifth player on a roller hockey team is the goalie. Goalies usually play defense. They guard their team's goal. Goalies rarely have the opportunity to take shots at the opposing team's goal.

The goalie's job is to prevent the opposing team from scoring. Goalies cannot stop every shot. But their job is to stop as many shots as possible. Goalies must be strong skaters. They must move quickly to collect loose pucks and to block shots.

Goalies must be tough, energetic, and limber. They play the entire game wearing heavy

Goalies must move quickly to collect loose pucks and block shots.

protective gear. Goalies also must have fast reflexes, good balance, and excellent eyesight to see and stop fast-moving pucks or balls.

Goalies try to stop shots any way they can. They block low shots with their skates, stick blades, and leg pads. Goalies must sometimes kick their legs out to stop a speeding puck or ball. Goalies use their goalkeeper's glove to catch high shots. They also use their blocker to deflect shots away from their goal.

Roller Hockey Rules

Roller hockey games have two equal periods. The length of each period is usually 15 minutes. But period length can vary depending on league rules.

Roller hockey games start with a face-off at the center circle. One player from each team stands in the circle during a face-off. A referee drops the puck between the two players. The two players then battle with their sticks for control of the puck or ball.

Once started, the game does not stop for player substitutions. Players enter and leave the rink during the action of the game. This method of substitution is called changing on the fly.

Roller hockey games start with a face-off.

Most games have a rest period between halves. Players call this rest period halftime. Halftime lasts about five minutes. Teams switch goals when halftime ends.

Roller Hockey Leagues

Today, several amateur leagues exist throughout North America and the world. An

Roller hockey is one of the fastest growing sports in North America.

amateur is a person who plays a sport for pleasure rather than money. There are amateur leagues for girls, boys, women, and men. There also are coed leagues. Coed means both men and women play on the same team.

Professional roller hockey began in 1993 when Roller Hockey International (RHI) formed. A professional roller hockey player receives money for taking part in the sport.

Professional roller hockey is basically the same as amateur roller hockey. But the two have some important differences. Professional players do not have to wear as much protective gear as amateur players. The rinks for professional roller hockey are larger than rinks for amateur roller hockey. Players have more physical contact in professional roller hockey. Amateur players are not allowed to check other players with their bodies.

Roller hockey is one of the fastest growing sports in North America. It is no longer just summer practice for ice hockey players. Roller hockey also is not just for professionals. The sport is for anyone who enjoys the thrill of skating and the excitement of hockey.

Words to Know

amateur (AM-uh-chur)—a person who plays a sport for pleasure rather than money

backhand (BAK-hand)—a shot or pass made with the back of a hockey stick's blade

cane (KANE)—a curved stick players use in field hockey

defender (di-FEND-ur)—a skater whose job is to prevent opposing skaters from scoring

flexible (FLEK-suh-buhl)—able to bend

forehand (FOR-hand)—a shot or pass players make with the front of a hockey stick's blade

forward (FOR-wurd)—a skater whose job is to move the puck or ball toward the opposing team's goal and score

goalie (GOH-lee)—a player who guards the goal and tries to prevent the opponent's shots from going into the net

professional (pruh-FESH-uh-nuhl)—a person who receives money for taking part in a sport

save (SAYV)—a stopped shot

stickhandling (STIK-hand-ling)—the ability to control and move a puck or ball with a hockey stick

To Learn More

Edwards, Chris. *The Young Inline Skater.* New York: Dorling Kindersley Publishing, 1996.

Mayo, Terry. *The Illustrated Rules of In-Line Hockey.* Nashville, Tenn.: Ideals Children's Books, 1996.

Millar, Cam. *Roller Hockey.* New York: Sterling Publishing, 1996.

Siller, Greg. *Roller Hockey: Skills and Strategies for Winning on Wheels.* Indianapolis: Masters Press, 1997.

Werner, Doug. *In-Line Skater's Start-Up: A Beginner's Guide to In-Line Skating and Roller Hockey.* Start-Up Sports. San Diego: Tracks Publishing, 1995.

Useful Addresses

Canadian Hockey Inline
2424 University Drive NW
Calgary, AB T2N 3Y9
Canada

**Canadian In-Line & Roller Skating
Association**
679 Queens Quay West
Unit 117
Toronto, ON M5V 3A9
Canada

USA Hockey InLine
4965 North 30th Street
Colorado Springs, CO 80919

**USA Roller Skating & The National
Museum of Roller Skating**
4730 South Street
P.O. Box 6579
Lincoln, NE 68506

Internet Sites

Black Ice
http://www.geocities.com/Colosseum/5296/
  index2.html

Canadian Hockey Inline
http://www.canadianhockeyinline.com/Whochi.html

Canadian In-Line & Roller Skating Association
http://home.ican.net/~cirsa/index.html

Major League Roller Hockey
http://www.mlrh.com/index2.html

Roller Hockey International
http://www.rollerhockey.com/index.html

USA Hockey InLine
http://www.inlinehockey.com/default.htm

USA Roller Skating—Roller Hockey
http://usacrs.com/roller.htm

Index